Mummy:
the inside story

Mummy:
the inside story

John H. Taylor

Harry N. Abrams, Inc., Publishers

BP is delighted to be able to sponsor *Mummy: the Inside Story* – a uniquely accessible exhibition which combines artistic, scientific and educational skills to tell the story of one individual ancient Egyptian. Non-invasive cutting-edge technology is used to uncover not only the wonders of ancient Egypt, but also to reveal and illuminate the secrets of one mummy, the priest Nesperennub, while leaving him undisturbed and untouched as he has been for nearly 3,000 years.

Lord Browne of Madingley
Group Chief Executive, BP

Library of Congress Control Number: 2004103904
ISBN 0–8109–9181–0

Originally published in Great Britain in 2004 by The British Museum Press.

Published in 2004 by Harry N. Abrams, Incorporated, New York.

Printed in Spain by Grafos S.A., Barcelona
10 9 8 7 6 5 4 3 2 1

Harry N. Abrams, Inc.
100 Fifth Avenue
New York, NY 10011
www.abramsbooks.com

J-Nf

Abrams is a subsidiary of
LA MARTINIÈRE
GROUPE

3 9547 00269 9143

CONTENTS

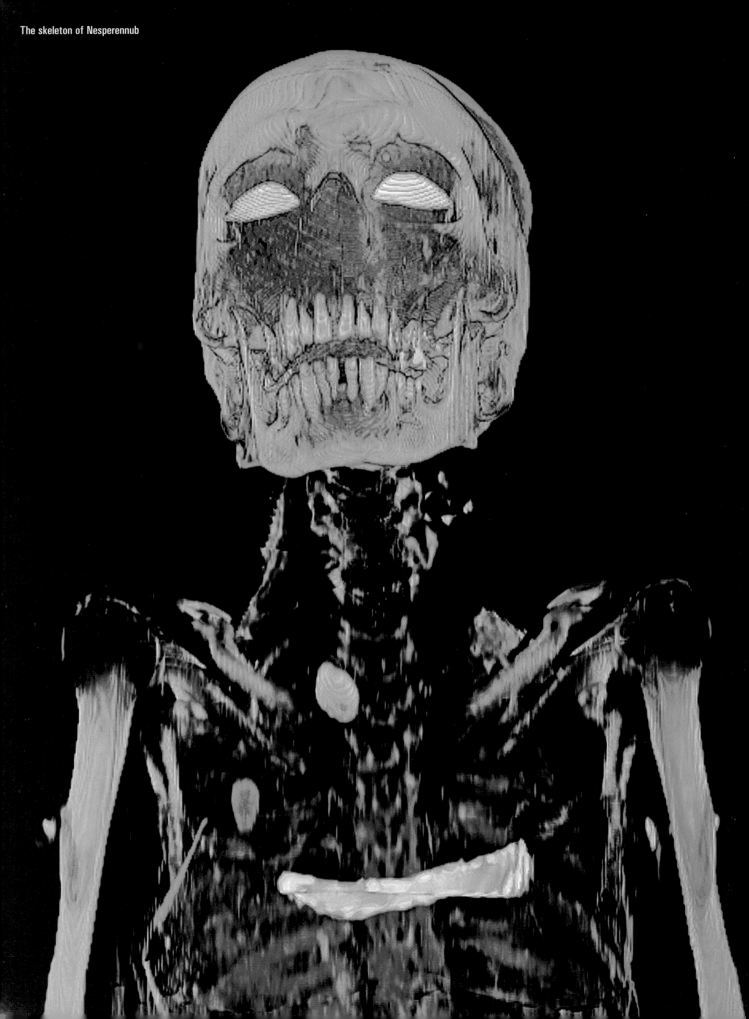

INTRODUCTION

Egyptian mummies are perennially popular with visitors to museums – but what is their relevance in the twenty-first century? What can we learn from the study of these ancient remains?

Mummies are an unparalleled source of scientific data, addressing a host of questions about life in one of the most highly-developed societies of the ancient world. Although the ancient Egyptians left many written records, these tell only part of the story, and researchers rely heavily on human remains to complete the picture. These throw light on many important issues about which the inscriptions are often silent: physical anthropology, family relationships, life expectancy, nutrition and health, disease and the causes of death. They also of course provide a unique insight into the fascinating and complex processes of mummification; including not only the artificial preservation of the corpse, but also the ritual elements which played such an important part: the placing of amulets, the putting on of wrappings and the equipping of the body with religious texts and images.

For many years, the only way to extract this data from Egyptian mummies was to unwrap them – a process both destructive and irreversible. Then, the advent of modern non-invasive imaging techniques – X-rays and Computerized Tomography (CT) scanning – made it possible to look inside a mummy without disturbing the wrappings in any way.

Now this technology has advanced still further. Thanks to the latest computer-generated images, we are able to perform a 'virtual unwrapping' of a mummy and to embark on a journey within the body, visualizing every feature and amulet in 3D. The subject chosen for this ground-breaking experiment, the priest Nesperennub, has been one of the British Museum's treasured exhibits for over a hundred years. His beautifully painted mummy-case has never been opened since it was sealed up by embalmers on the West Bank at Thebes shortly before he was buried, but now after 2,800 years technology has unlocked its secrets. The wealth of images that have been captured in this way have already proved valuable to researchers, and will bring museum visitors face to face with a man from the remote past in a unique and fascinating way.

This book takes the reader on a journey of discovery, gathering information about Nesperennub from a variety of sources. First, his place in history and his role in Egyptian society are pieced together from the inscriptions – the formal record of his life which was intended for posterity. Then the 3D technology makes it possible to enter the mummy case and to explore the body, collecting data about Nesperennub as a person, seeing his face, assessing his health, and looking over the shoulders of the embalmers as they prepared him for eternal life.

THE DISCOVERY OF NESPERENNUB

Nesperennub's body, enclosed in a cartonnage (linen and plaster) case and a wooden coffin, is an excellent specimen of Egyptian mummification practices in the Twenty-second and Twenty-third Dynasties (c.945–715 BC). It was discovered at Luxor, the site of the ancient city of Thebes, in the 1890s and bought by E.A. Wallis Budge on one of his regular visits to Egypt to collect antiquities for the British Museum. The mummy and its cases were sent to England by the shipping company Moss of Alexandria in 1899.

Nesperennub's burial had probably been found by local diggers in a tomb on the West Bank at Thebes, but Budge left no record of its exact location. It is unlikely that he was ever shown the find *in situ*; the local dealers who acted as suppliers of antiquities were often reticent about revealing their sources. During the ninth and eighth centuries BC, when Nesperennub lived, many of the citizens of Thebes were buried in the sepulchres of officials of the New Kingdom (c.1550–1069 BC) – the 'tombs of the nobles', whose brilliantly painted chapels in the cliffs facing the Nile are among the spots most visited by today's tourists. Although many of these tombs were then five, six or seven centuries old, they were still in use, ownership often passing from one family to another. Mummies were interred either in the burial chambers of the original occupants of the tombs, or at the bottom of shafts newly cut below the courtyards or chapels. Sometimes mummies were placed in the painted chapel itself, which was then sealed up. Alternatively, entirely new tombs were being constructed within the enclosures of temples along the edge of the Nile floodplain. But burials found there are generally less well-preserved than those from the New Kingdom tombs higher up in the cliffs; the excellent preservation of Nesperennub's coffins may indicate that he was interred in one of these older tombs.

Together with Nesperennub's mummy, the British Museum also purchased another coffin, inscribed for a man named Ankhefenkhons. Wallis Budge identified this man as the father of Nesperennub, and the inscriptions on their coffins support this. It is probable, then, that the

LEFT The mummy of Nesperennub in its cartonnage case. British Museum EA 30720.

RIGHT Tombs of the New Kingdom at Qurna on the West Bank at Thebes.

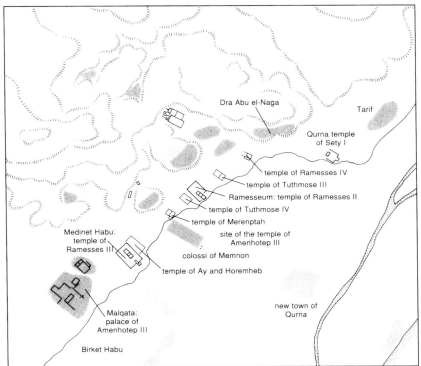

burial place, wherever it was, accommodated several members of the same family. The mummy of Ankhefenkhons has not come to light, but in the nineteenth century objects that were found together were frequently offered for sale to different collectors, so the body might have been purchased by someone other than Budge. This is all the more likely because between 1899 and 1905 the American Egyptologist George Reisner, acting on behalf of Phoebe Apperson Hearst, bought another set of coffins which probably came from the same family-tomb. These are now in the Hearst Museum of Anthropology at the University of California, Berkeley. The inscriptions identify the owner as the lady Neskhonspakhered, and she is described as the wife of Nesperennub, son of Ankhefenkhons. The husband is credited with the same priestly titles as the British Museum's Nesperennub, and any doubt that Neskhonspakhered was married to him is dispelled at a glance, as both husband and wife have matching

coffins, clearly made and painted by the same craftsmen. They must have been ordered at around the same time. Unfortunately, the mummy of Neskhonspakhered is also missing; perhaps it was sold to another collector, or left behind in Egypt.

9

READING THE HIEROGLYPHS (1):

The hieroglyphic inscriptions on the coffins of Nesperennub and his family provide basic information which enable us to locate him in time and place. Typically, this data occurs in the context of standardized religious formulae, and gives us only Nesperennub's official titles and the names of his relatives. Nothing is disclosed about the personalities of the people concerned, their lifespans, or anything touching on the times in which they lived.

The inscription on the lid of Nesperennub's wooden coffin reads: *An offering which the king gives to Ra-Horakhty-Atum, the lord of the two lands and of Heliopolis, [to] Ptah-Sokar-Osiris, the lord of the shetayet-shrine, [and to] Wennefer, the ruler of eternity, [in order that they] might give life, prosperity and health to the Beloved of the God, the Opener of the Doors of Heaven in Karnak, the Libationer of Khons of Benenet, Nesper[en]nub, son of the like-titled Ankhefenkhons, justified.*

The text on the front of the cartonnage case provides much the same information in an abbreviated form: *An offering which the king gives to Osiris, so that he might give life to the Beloved of the God, the Libationer of Khons of* Benenet, *Nesperennub, son of the like-titled Ankhefenkhons, justified.*

These inscriptions reveal that Nesperennub and his father worked in the great religious complex of Karnak, the cult-centre of the god Amun-Ra. This deity was the supreme god of the Egyptian state, and was the senior figure of a 'holy family', the other members of which were the goddess Mut, wife of Amun-Ra, and the god Khons, their son. The father and mother deities each had a complete temple-

FAR LEFT Inscription on the lid of the outer coffin of Nesperennub. British Museum EA 30720.

ABOVE Name and titles of Nesperennub, from his cartonnage mummy-case. British Museum EA 30720.

LEFT Reconstruction of the city of Thebes, about 1100 BC, looking from the temples of Karnak towards the tombs on the west bank of the Nile.

NESPERENNUB'S PLACE IN SOCIETY

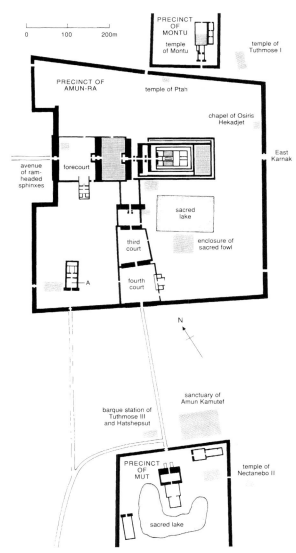

LEFT The temple of Amun-Re at Karnak, looking north-west across the Sacred Lake.

BELOW Plan of the temples of Karnak.
A = temple of Khons.

complex of their own at Karnak. The temple of Khons (called *Benenet* by the ancient Egyptians) was situated in the south-west corner of the complex of Amun-Ra.

Khons was a very ancient deity who was associated with the moon. His name, which means 'wanderer', refers to the moon's passage across the night sky, and he is usually depicted wearing a lunar disc and crescent as his headdress. Khons is often shown with the head of a falcon, but when his role as the child of Amun and Mut is emphasized he usually appears in fully human form, shaven-headed except for a curled sidelock and often holding one finger to his lips – both standard conventions used by Egyptian artists to represent a child.

Nesperennub may have served in the temple of Amun-Ra, but it appears that he was mainly associated with the cult of Khons. His links with that priesthood are further emphasized by an inscription found on the roof-terrace of the temple of Khons (p. 13). This text was carved for a man named Nebetkheper, who was the son of Nesperennub. The inscription is dated to the seventh year of the reign of Takelot III of the Twenty-third Dynasty (*c.*750 BC), a ruler of a local, Theban-based royal line which controlled southern Upper Egypt as a semi-independent principality. The inscription supplements the data from the coffins by recording other titles held by Nesperennub (pp. 13–14). It also includes a long pedigree, listing many of his ancestors; this information can be compared with the genealogical data from the coffin of his father Ankhefenkhons (pp. 14–15). All of this written evidence makes clear that Nesperennub was a man of high status and a member of a clan which had wielded influence at Thebes for many years.

READING THE HIEROGLYPHS (2):

We know that Nesperennub belonged to a long-established family of priests. In earlier periods, priestly duties were performed by ordinary citizens for a specified time, but from the New Kingdom (c.1550–1069 BC) it was customary for people to serve as 'full-time' priests. The roles of the priests became diversified. Each office carried a stipend and brought with it specific duties – though in practice these were rarely onerous.

Posts were hereditary, and it was common for particular families to serve in the same temple for many generations. At the same time, an individual could 'collect' offices, entitling him to carry out a variety of duties in different temples. The more junior priests worked on a shift-basis, rotating on and off duty in groups. While their term of office lasted, they were obliged to observe regulations relating to purity: they had to bathe in the temple lake, have their heads shaved, abstain from sexual contacts and follow dietary restrictions and a dress code.

Some priestly titles were indications of rank. This perhaps applies to Nesperennub's 'Beloved of the God', a common title of Theban priests at the time, but one which does not seem to have carried clearly-defined duties. Others were connected to the daily ritual which was carried out in every temple. The temple served as an earthly home for the god, whose spirit was believed to animate the 'cult image' – a statue made of precious metal, which was

FAR LEFT Bronze statuette of the god Khons. The curled sidelock and the position of the right hand, with finger to lip, signify his youthfulness. On his head is the moon in two forms, full disc and crescent, and above that a crown adorned with ram's horns and ostrich feathers. Late Period, about 600 BC. British Museum EA 35418.

BELOW Entrance to the temple of Khons at Karnak.

NESPERENNUB THE PRIEST

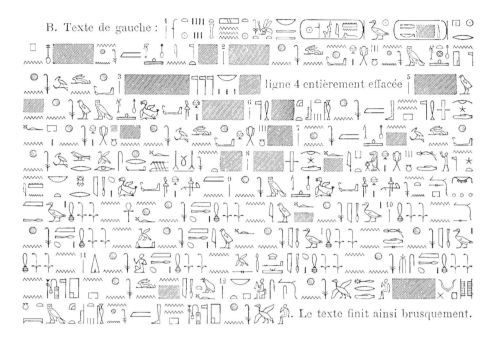

B. Texte de gauche :

ligne 4 entièrement effacée

Le texte finit ainsi brusquement.

kept in the sanctuary, or holy-of-holies. Every day, the shrine containing the god's image was opened. It was purified and clothed and nourishment was offered to it. Nesperennub's title 'Opener of the Doors of Heaven' indicates that he performed part of this ritual: his job was to open the doors of the shrine. The revelation of the god each morning was likened to the rising of the sun into the sky at dawn – a moment that for the Egyptians symbolized the renewal of all life and creation. Other priests then burned incense and performed the god's toilet and feeding. This part of the ritual involved the pouring of libations to purify the god's dwelling and his meal. The coffin inscriptions show that here too Nesperennub played his role, sprinkling water from a tall libation-jar over the offering table in front of the cult-statue.

The inscription from the Karnak temple gives Nesperennub the title 'Fan-bearer on the right hand of Khons'. This role would be performed at religious festivals at specified times of the year. The image of Khons, mounted on a miniature barque (boat), would be brought out of his temple and carried in procession on the shoulders of priests. Others would carry fans to create a breeze and drive away flies. These processions were rare opportunities for the ordinary citizens of Thebes to approach closely to the gods.

READING THE HIEROGLYPHS (3):

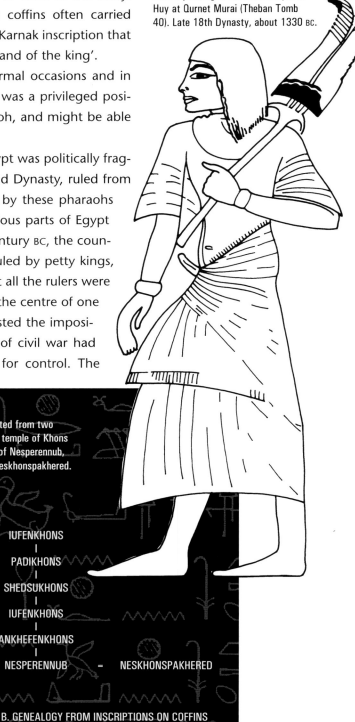

Priestly duties would not occupy all of Nesperennub's time. Many priests also held secular offices alongside their religious functions. These were often posts in the administration or even in the army. Nesperennub was no exception, but because coffins often carried predominantly religious titles it is only from the Karnak inscription that we learn that he was 'Fan-bearer on the right hand of the king'.

The fanbearers attended on the king on formal occasions and in processions. Despite its rather menial sound, it was a privileged position. Fanbearers had direct access to the pharaoh, and might be able to exert an influence over royal policy.

At the time in which Nesperennub lived, Egypt was politically fragmented. The main royal line, the Twenty-second Dynasty, ruled from Tanis in the Delta, but the territory controlled by these pharaohs had shrunk over the years as local rulers in various parts of Egypt became virtually independent. By the eighth century BC, the country had become a patchwork of states, some ruled by petty kings, others by chiefs of Libyan tribes – indeed almost all the rulers were of Libyan extraction at this period. Thebes was the centre of one of these states. The powerful officials there resisted the imposition of authority from the north, and periods of civil war had even occurred, with rival factions competing for control. The

Nesperennub's family-tree, as reconstructed from two different sources: A, inscription from the temple of Khons at Karnak; B, inscriptions on the coffins of Nesperennub, his father Ankhefenkhons and his wife Neskhonspakhered.

WENEN ...
|
KHONSMOSE
|
PAESAAKHAU
|
DIKHONS
|
SHEDSUKHONS
|
IUFENKHONS   IUFENKHONS
| |
PADIKHONS   PADIKHONS
| |
NESKHONS   SHEDSUKHONS
| |
IUFENKHONS   IUFENKHONS
| |
ANKHEFENKHONS   KHONSPAKHERED   ANKHEFENKHONS
| |
NESPERENNUB = NESKHONSPAKHERED   NESPERENNUB = NESKHONSPAKHERED
|
NEBETKHEPER

A. GENEALOGY FROM KARNAK INSCRIPTION   B. GENEALOGY FROM INSCRIPTIONS ON COFFINS

NESPERENNUB'S SECULAR ROLE AND FAMILY

post of high priest of Amun was of key importance and became the focus of bitter conflict. By the end of the ninth century BC, Thebes had thrown off allegiance to the kings at Tanis and instead recognized the authority of a line of rulers now called the Twenty-third Dynasty. The longest-reigning of these kings was Osorkon III (c.780 BC) and it was probably in his time that Nesperennub lived, since the inscription of his son Nebetkheper was carved in the reign of the next pharaoh, Takelot III.

Nesperennub's family

Family ties were of great importance in the everyday lives of the ancient Egyptians. Marriage, with the procreation of many children, was the aspiration of most people. Property – whether land, movable goods or lucrative offices – was passed from generation to generation, and children were expected in their turn to provide for the burial and funerary cult of their dead parents. The recording of genealogies helped to establish hereditary claims to property on earth and to priestly or official titles.

From the Karnak inscription and from the coffins of Nesperennub, Ankhefenkhons and Neskhonspakhered, an extensive genealogy can be reconstructed (p. 14). This shows that the family had been attached to the cult of Khons for centuries, and that their titles had been passed from father to son for many generations. The sources are in complete agreement about the sequence of names except at one point; Nesperennub's great-grandfather is named in the coffin texts as Shedsukhons, but in the Karnak inscription he is called Neskhons. These two names could easily be confused when written in hieroglyphs. There are two possible explanations. As this section of the Karnak inscription is heavily damaged, the name may simply have been misread by Georges Daressy, the French Egyptologist who copied and published it in the 1890s. Alternatively, one of the ancient scribes who wrote the original texts may himself have made a mistake; such confusions occur quite often in repetitive genealogical texts.

Nesperennub's wife came from another family which held office in the same temple. Her name, Neskhonspakhered, means 'She who belongs to Khons the Child', and her father was a Libation-priest of Khons, as well as a shrine-opener and temple scribe. This intermarriage of the son and daughter of two professional colleagues is an indication of the close-knit world of the priests, and the influence of the temple on their daily lives.

RIGHT Cartonnage mummy-case of Neskhonspakhered, wife of Nesperennub. Phoebe A. Hearst Museum, Berkeley, California, 6-19929. This case is decorated in a style similar to that of Nesperennub himself. Both husband and wife also possessed almost identical outer wooden coffins which were probably made in the same craftsmen's workshop.

GATHERING DATA FROM MUMMIES

Egyptologists are fortunate in having an enormous amount of written evidence with which to reconstruct ancient Egyptian life and culture. The walls of tombs and temples were covered with hieroglyphic inscriptions, while rolls of papyrus, preserved almost pristine by the dry climate, contain often lengthy texts written in ink. But most of these writings are formal in character. Temple inscriptions and funerary texts reflect a stable and perfect world, in which all was controlled according to *Maat*, the ideal state of order.

ABOVE Invitation to the 'unrolling' of an Egyptian mummy in London, 1850.

OPPOSITE LEFT Full-body radiograph of a Theban mummy of the 22nd Dynasty, X-rayed as part of a general survey of mummies at the British Museum in the 1960s. Preserved internal organs and dense packing materials are visible within the chest and between the legs.

OPPOSITE RIGHT CT image of the mummy of Tjentmutengebtiu from Thebes, about 900 BC. This cross-section through the cartonnage-case shows the layers of linen wrappings, the chest and arm-bones, and objects inside the body.

BELOW Margaret Murray (1863–1963) and her team at the unwrapping of the mummy of one of the 'Two Brothers' at Manchester, 1908. Although this investigation was ahead of its time in pioneering a multi-disciplinary approach, the destructive effect of unwrapping is clearly apparent.

The day to day realities were different. The Egyptians constantly battled natural and socio-political problems – famine and disease, economic stress and civil unrest. Such things did not fit with the concept of *Maat*, and mention of them is usually excluded from the formal inscriptions. Although some written sources throw light on these matters, they are rare and are unevenly distributed throughout the 3,000-year span of ancient Egyptian history.

The mummy of Nesperennub and its painted cases perfectly exemplify the dichotomy of the historian's sources. The mummiform coffins present us with idealized images of their occupant as young, handsome and healthy. The inscriptions proclaim his probity on earth through official titles indicating status and responsibility, and the paintings are reassuring indications that all will go well for him in the hereafter. The mummy within the coffins reveals much that is not expressed elsewhere, about physical anthropology, life expectancy, nutrition, health, disease, manner of death, and mummification processes – the realities of existence, which often could not be fully controlled and may have been far from the ideal. It is through examining the human remains that personal stories of life in the society of ancient Egypt can be revealed.

For many years, the only way to extract information from mummies was to unwrap them. In the early nineteenth century, mummy 'unrollings' were often dramatic performances, carried out before fee-paying audiences drawn from the fashionable elements of European society. Although there was some gain in knowledge, invasive study had many disadvantages: irreversible damage to the body and wrappings, the loss of the context of all objects found within the bandages, and sometimes the

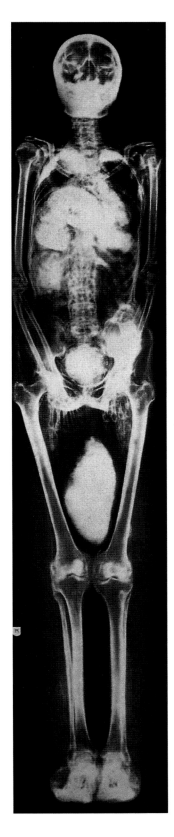

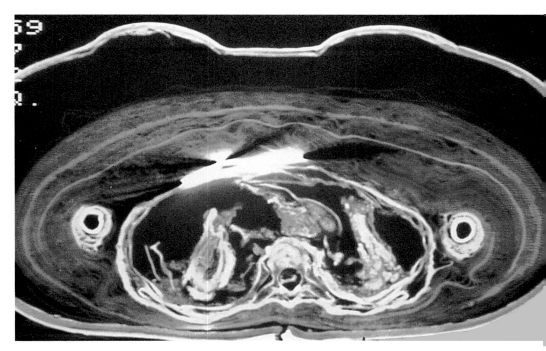

complete destruction of the mummy. Once a mummy has been unwrapped, much of its value as a time capsule is lost for ever. The original assemblage of evidence cannot be revisited to answer any new questions that may arise.

Non-invasive imaging has transformed this picture. The potential of X-rays for investigating Egyptian mummies was realized as early as the 1890s, and hundreds of mummies were X-rayed during the twentieth century. However, these images, created by projecting a single beam of radiation through the mummy, were not always clear. Anatomical structures and objects are superimposed on the X-ray plate, making them difficult to distinguish. The solidified resin and other dense materials inside mummies also impaired the clarity of the image. These problems were overcome by the development of CT (Computerized Tomography) scanning. The method involves passing X-ray beams through the body from different angles. This eliminates the difficulty of superimposed images and enables the data to be used with greater versatility. CT data can be displayed on a computer screen as a series of two-dimensional axial 'slices' through the body. This presents to the viewer everything within the object scanned. Different structures are distinguished according to their relative density on a scale from black (minimum density), through grey, to white (maximum density). Features of specific and consistent densities (such as bone, ceramic or metal) can also be selected and displayed in the form of 3D images. Thus from the scanning of a mummy, a skull or individual bones can be isolated. Such reconstructions can even be animated to create a 'fly-through' (see pp.18–19). Thanks to this method, the unwrapping of mummies has become rare, and imaging technology continues to break new barriers.

IMAGING NESPERENNUB:

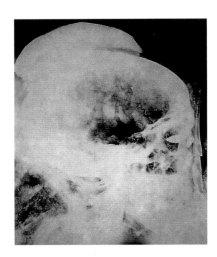

In 2000, a chance meeting led to an exciting collaboration between the British Museum and Silicon Graphics Inc. (SGI). SGI, a maker of powerful supercomputers, already had an impressive record in the creation and visualisation of highly complex computerized datasets; in fields as varied as the oil industry, diagnostic medicine, car design and public education projects such as planetarium presentations.

The mummy of Nesperennub was CT scanned at a London hospital, and over 1,500 cross-sectional images were obtained at 1mm intervals. Using a powerful visual supercomputer (an Onyx Infinite Reality), SGI specialists reassembled all of the image 'slices' into a single 3D 'volumetric' dataset that can be viewed and explored interactively using a technique called 'real-time volume rendering'.

An SGI software toolset called OpenGL Volumizer allows the user to view the image from any angle, and to adjust numerous parameters such as density and opacity to display different layers and structures and to tease out fine detail buried deep in the body. A 'clipping plane', passed through any axis to remove sections of the dataset that the viewer does not wish to see, can act as a 'virtual scalpel', slicing cleanly through the body and exposing a cross-section of what is inside. Artificial lighting casts shadows that help to interpret the shape of

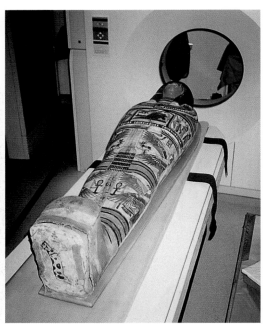

TOP Conventional X-ray of the head of Nesperennub, made in the 1960s. The cloudy image shows only that artificial eyes are present and that there is a dense object on the top of the skull (*cf.* pp. 38–9).

ABOVE The mummy of Nesperennub, still sealed inside its painted case, enters the CT scanner at the National Hospital for Neurology and Neurosurgery, London.

RIGHT Cross-sectional CT image of Nesperennub, looking towards the head. Bundles and strands of cloth, some of which contain the embalmed internal organs, are visible inside the chest. These are partly embedded in a fluid (probably resin) which had solidified after being poured into the body.

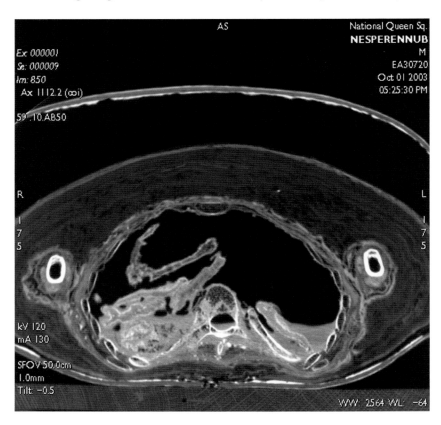

NEW TECHNOLOGY

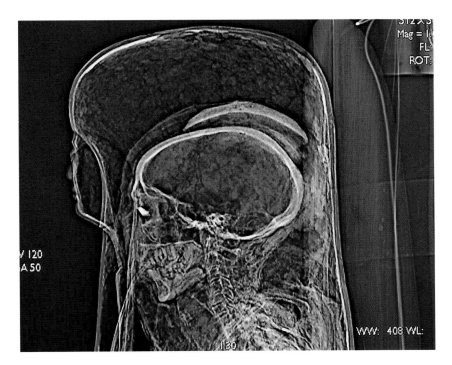

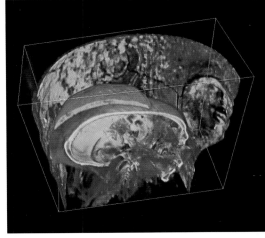

ABOVE A virtual reality theatre, in which 3D images can be projected on to a curved screen and manipulated using a supercomputer.

LEFT Lateral topogram, or CT scout film, showing the body of Nesperennub. The skull is positioned at a lower level than the face of the mummy-case with an empty space above. This indicates that the case was made to a standard size, rather than being built up around the mummy itself (*cf.* pp. 42–3).

bones or objects. By changing the observer's viewpoint, the operator can fly closer to the body and even travel *inside* the data, giving the illusion of being under the wrappings and even within the body itself. The study of Nesperennub represents the first time that this technology has been applied to a complete body interactively.

All of this is executed in '3D stereo', where the computer supplies a slightly different image to the left and right eyes via a special set of glasses, displaying the mummy in true 3D. This is not just realistic, but also very useful when trying to interpret what is inside the mummy.

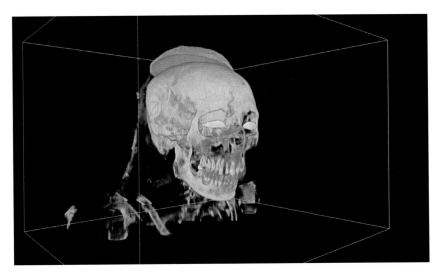

ABOVE A volume of data can be viewed from any angle on the screen. 'Clipping planes' enable a section to be cut through the block of data at any point and at any angle required.

LEFT The skeleton of Nesperennub projected in 3D stereo on the screen in a virtual reality theatre. In this image, the computer has been instructed to display only structures of relatively high density, such as stone, bone and ceramic.

A TOUR OF THE MUMMY

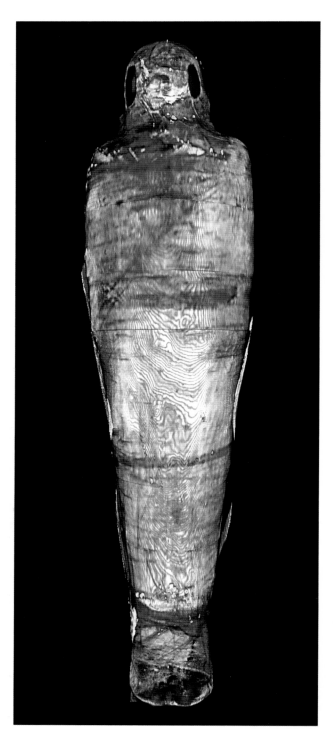

These four images demonstrate how the 3D data can be used to perform a 'virtual unwrapping' of the mummy of Nesperennub. Any feature inside or outside the body can be revealed and scrutinized in detail.

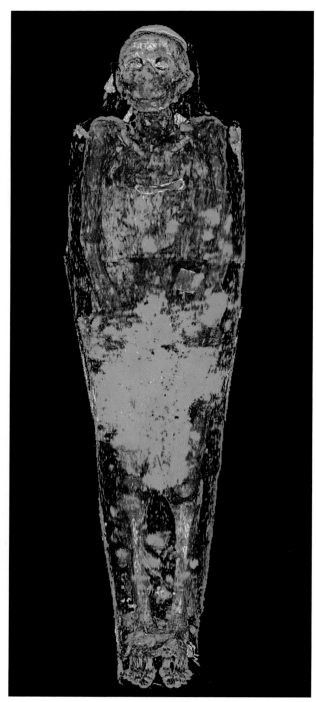

ABOVE The mummy in its outer linen wrappings.

RIGHT The wrappings removed to reveal the remains of soft tissues.

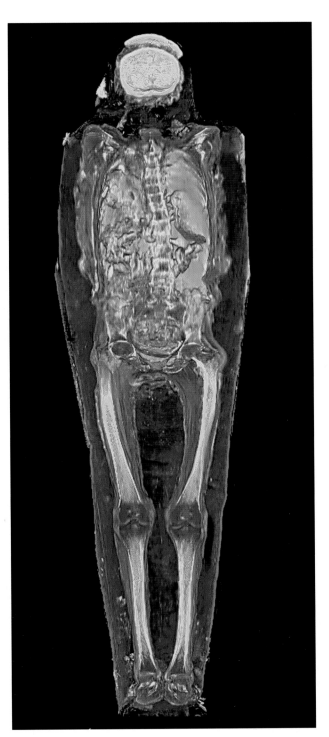

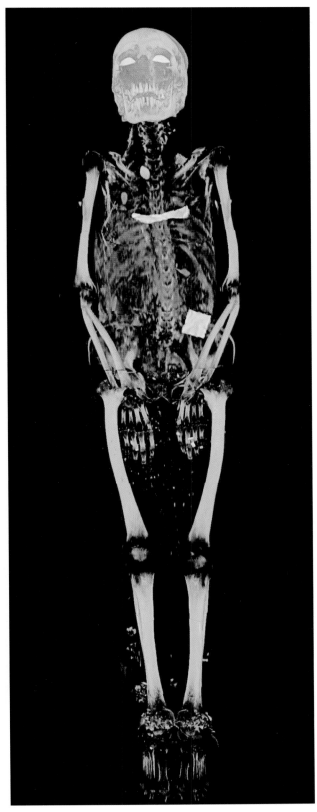

ABOVE Cross-section through the body showing interior of skull and chest cavity.

RIGHT The skeleton; objects of dense materials are also visible.

SOFT TISSUE PRESERVATION:

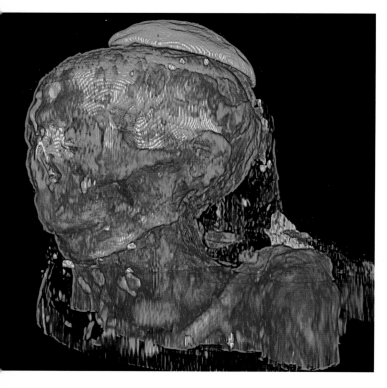

When a body was mummified, the head was treated with special care. It was thought to be important that the dead person should have the use of their eyes, ears, nose and mouth, just as they had done in life. Also a lifelike rendering of the face was considered an essential element of the transfigured corpse. At some periods a mask was placed over the wrappings of the mummy, showing the deceased in an idealized manner. But at the time of Nesperennub, more attention was paid to making the actual face appear lifelike beneath the bandages. This was often done by inserting packing materials such as linen, sand, mud or sawdust under the skin to fill out the shrunken features. There are signs that Nesperennub's body was treated in this way; some areas (particularly the throat) have clearly been stuffed with some unidentifiable material.

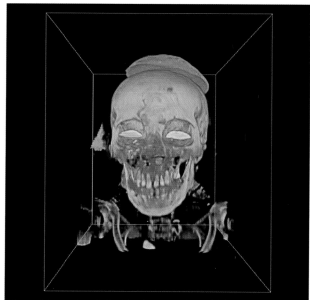

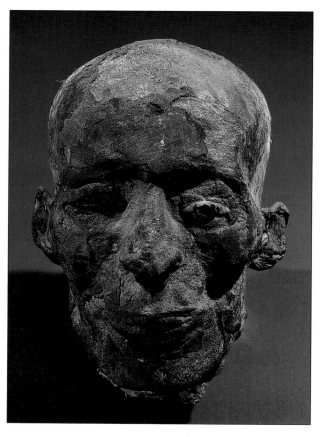

TOP The face of Nesperennub.

ABOVE Artificial eyes in the orbits of Nesperennub's skull.

RIGHT Unwrapped head of a male mummy with artificial eye *in situ*. Third Intermediate Period, about 1070–664 BC. British Museum EA 67815.

THE FACE OF NESPERENNUB

It was also common for the body to be painted (red for men, yellow for women) to resemble a statue, and for artificial eyes to be put into the eye sockets.

The 3D images show that the soft tissues of Nesperennub's face are well preserved, the nose, mouth and ears all clearly visible. Artificial eyes are present in the orbits. They are made of a dense material, perhaps stone or opaque glass. No hair can be seen, but this may have been shaved off before death as part of the bodily purification which Nesperennub was obliged to undergo when fulfilling his duties as a priest. Soft tissue is well-preserved throughout the whole body, including hands, feet, fingers, toes and genitals.

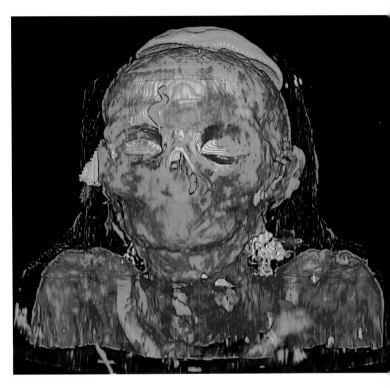

RIGHT The face of Nesperennub. The mouth is concealed by a thick application of resin.

BELOW The feet of Nesperennub, showing the excellent preservation of the toes and nails.

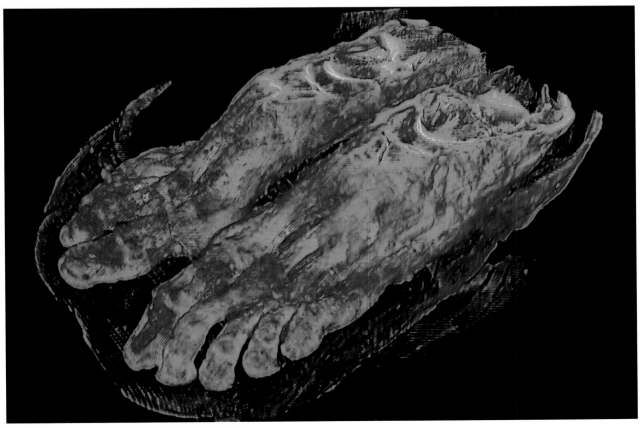

NESPERENNUB'S APPEARANCE:

Using skulls, it is possible to reconstruct the living appearance of people from the past. Standard techniques for this have been perfected in police work, where it is often necessary to identify decomposed bodies, and the same process can be applied to ancient remains. Pegs are attached to the skull (or to a replica of the skull) at specific points. These indicate the depth of soft tissue usually present at those locations on the human head. With these pegs as reference-points, muscles, eyes and skin are modelled using clay and attached to the skull. When the process is complete, artificial colouring can be applied to the skin and eyes, and hair added to produce a realistic impression. The bone structure, of course, does not determine

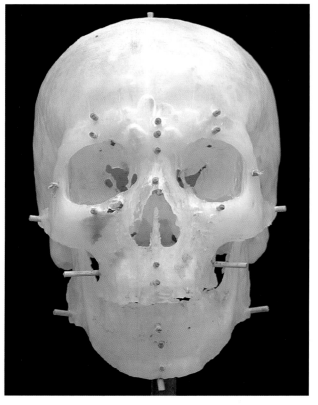

every contour of the soft tissues, and so a reconstruction of this kind can never be one hundred percent accurate. None the less, it generally provides a recognizable likeness of the individual.

This procedure can even be followed when the skull is physically inaccessible within the wrappings of a mummy. The CT scans are first accessed and the data relating to structures made of bone selected; some manual 'editing' of the data is necessary to remove desiccated skin and other dense materials which could be confused with bone. A stereolithographic replica of the skull is then made in resin.

Nesperennub's skull has features commonly found among ancient Egyptian men. His lower jaw is notably substantial. The reconstruction takes account of his age as estimated from the state of his skeleton, and he is shown without hair, as befitted a priest.

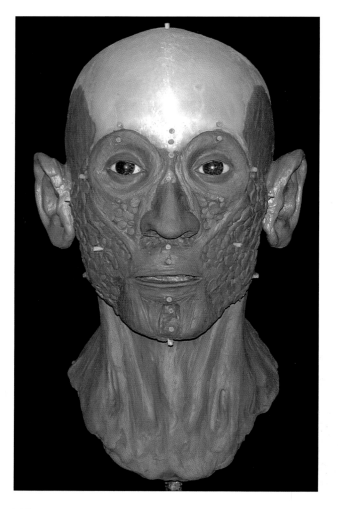

FACIAL RECONSTRUCTION

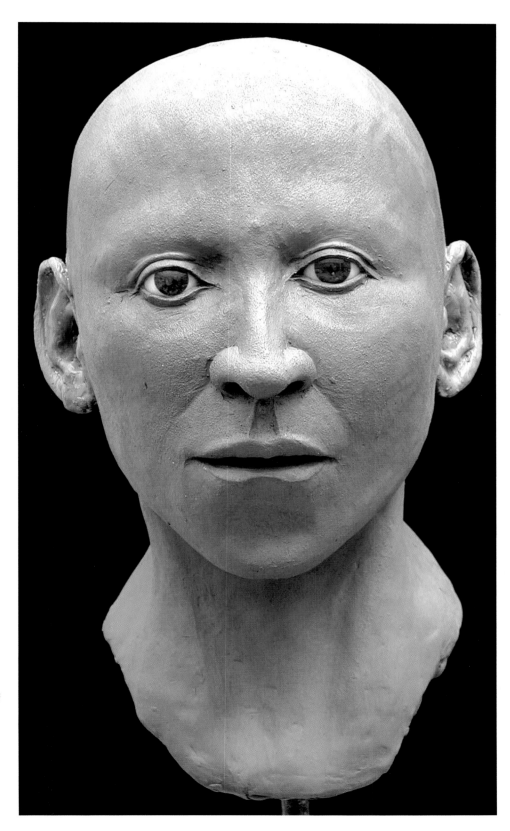

OPPOSITE TOP Facsimile of Nesperennub's skull, modelled from CT data. Pegs have been attached to indicate the depth of soft tissue usually present at specific points on the skull.

OPPOSITE BOTTOM Head with muscles, eyes and ears added.

RIGHT Nesperennub's probable appearance in life: clay head with artificial eyes inserted.

AGE AT DEATH

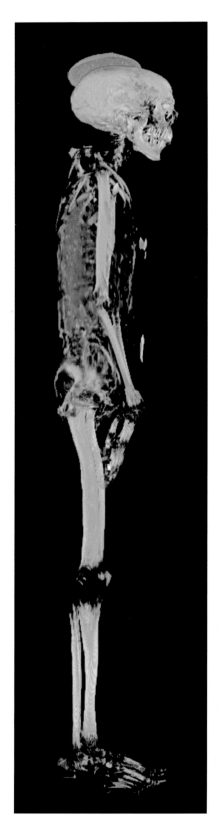

Although the ancient Egyptians were keenly aware of the passage of human life (and regarded 110 years as the ideal age to attain), inscriptions in tombs and on coffins very rarely provide details of the age at which the occupant died. It is the bodies, and above all else, the skeletal remains which offer clues to the age. The development of the teeth and the growth of bones follow a pattern which allows osteologists to estimate the stage of life which an individual had reached, although allowance must be made for regional variations in these growth-rates. Once a person has reached adulthood, the fusing of parts of the skeleton prevents further growth; so for older individuals the main clues to age are in the degenerative changes that advancing age brings: wear on or loss of teeth, changes in the bones of the skull, the vertebrae and the ribs, and signs of wear on joints.

The X-rays made in the 1960s, showed that Nesperennub was a full adult. Dawson and Gray estimated his age at thirty to forty years old. This figure was probably deduced from the state of his teeth, which they regarded as moderately worn. The more recent assessment shows that his teeth are well worn, yet no other major problems are visible, except what may be an abscess (p 28). The bony plates that form the skull are almost fully joined, an indication that he was a mature adult. Yet the sutures which mark the points at which the plates fuse are still clearly visible and, as these become progressively less obvious with advancing age, it is unlikely that Nesperennub was an elderly man.

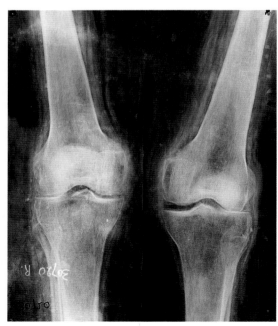

FAR LEFT Full-length view of the skeleton of Nesperennub.

LEFT X-ray of the leg-bones. Above and below the knee-joints are faint horizontal lines ('Harris lines') which are indications that Nesperennub underwent periods of arrested growth during his earlier life.

The spine, which often shows traces of age-related change and deterioration, appears to be in fairly good condition. There is some osteoarthritis, a build-up of extra bony material at the extremities of the vertebrae. This is a common sign of ageing, yet it is not pronounced in this case. These factors taken together suggest that Nesperennub died when he was middle-aged. We cannot accurately assess how many years he lived, but forty would probably be close to the truth. Life expectancy in ancient Egypt was much lower than it is today. Many infectious diseases and minor injuries, now easily treatable, were fatal then, and the average age at death for men was thirty-five, so Nesperennub would not have considered his lifespan unduly short.

Lines are visible at the ends of the tibiae. These so-called 'Harris lines' are the marks left on the bones by a temporary interruption of the growth process. Periods of illness or nutritional stress are believed to be the cause. The fact that Nesperennub had several of these lines suggests that during his earlier life, when his skeleton was maturing, he either suffered illness or experienced spells of poor diet. Harris lines have been detected in many Egyptian skeletons, even those of persons who were wealthy enough to afford elaborate mummification. It remains uncertain whether these episodes are related to disease or to fluctuations in the food supply from such factors as bad harvests, famine or economic instability.

Once Nesperennub was fully grown and had begun his career as a priest, he would have enjoyed a privileged lifestyle. He would not have had to do hard, manual work – as the absence of broken or fractured bones in his skeleton shows – but would have lived in relative comfort. His diet would have been a healthy and well-balanced one – mainly bread, fruit and vegetables, with beer or wine to drink. He would also have had more meat to eat than the average peasant. Beef and poultry were among the regular offerings made in the temples, and once the god had been satisfied his priests were allowed to dine on what remained.

ABOVE Back view of the skull. The bony plates are united but the sutures are still visible (centre), suggesting that Nesperennub was a mature but not elderly man at the time of his death.

BELOW All Nesperennub's teeth are present, with the exception of his third molars (wisdom teeth). This supports the notion that he died before reaching old age.

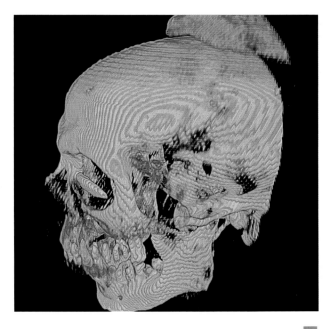

DENTAL HEALTH

Teeth

The ancient Egyptians suffered from many dental problems. The contamination of their food by wind-blown sand caused extensive wear on the biting surfaces of the teeth, leading to infections and abscesses. Dental surgery was not practiced – only pharmaceutical remedies being available – and unrelieved toothache must have been widespread.

Nesperennub's teeth were generally in good condition. All of them appear to be present except for the third molars (wisdom teeth) – but often these do not erupt. There is quite heavy wear on the biting surfaces of the teeth. This might in some places have exposed the roots and allowed infection to enter. There is at least one place on Nesperennub's lower jaw where this seems to have happened; a cavity is apparent at the root of the first molar on the right-hand side. This might be explained as an example of resorption (the retraction of the bony setting of the tooth), but in view

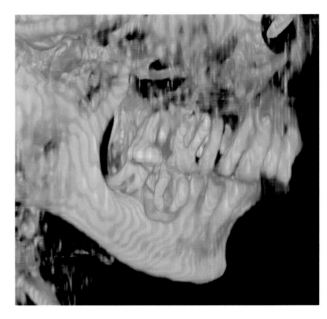

of the heavy wear already mentioned it is more likely to be a dental abscess. It would certainly have caused Nesperennub much pain and discomfort, and probably made him irritable and short-tempered.

Evidence of disease?

Nesperennub's skeleton is complete, with no broken bones or signs of major trauma. However, there is one curious anomaly on his skull. The 3D images of show a small cavity or hole in the bone, above the left eye. This hole is not easy to explain. It does not have any connection with the process of mummification; the brain was usually extracted via the nose, and there is no reason to doubt that this was done in the case of Nesperennub. There are no traces of cracking or splitting of the bone, as might be expected if the hole had been caused by a blow or a wound with a sharp instrument or weapon.

A third possibility is that Nesperennub had suffered from an illness which attacked the bone of his skull. The axial CT images show that the abnormal cavity mainly affected the interior of the skull, and that the bone was not completely pierced. This

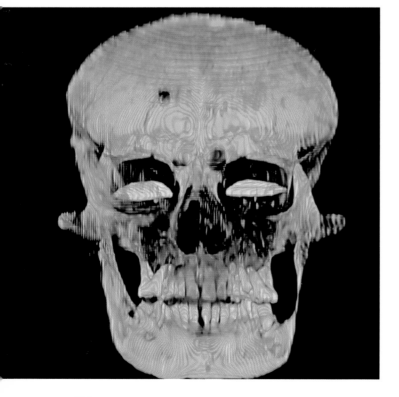

AND A CAVITY IN THE SKULL

would suggest that the damage came from inside. If it is not a healed injury, then some form of tumour might have been responsible. After the brain had been removed during mummification, the only trace of the condition remaining would be this mark on the bone.

If this hypothesis is correct, the illness would almost certainly have contributed to Nesperennub's death. No suitable medical treatment would have been available to the doctors of his time. The Edwin Smith Surgical Papyrus, one of the most important medical treatises to survive from ancient Egypt, records remedies that were thought appropriate for certain head injuries (such as a broken nose), but less straightforward conditions were considered untreatable.

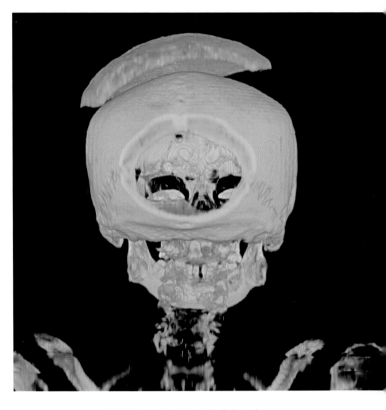

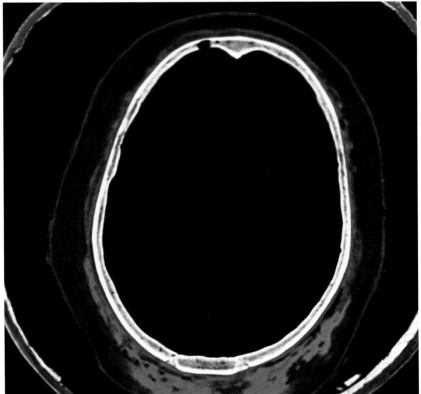

ABOVE View into the skull through a clipping plane, showing small abnormal cavity above the left eye socket.

LEFT CT image of the skull showing the cavity above the eye. This view shows that it had almost pierced the frontal bone of the skull.

OPPOSITE TOP Detail of the right side of the jaws, showing signs of an abscess at the root of the first lower molar.

OPPOSITE BOTTOM View of the interior of the skull showing Nesperennub's well-preserved teeth.

MUMMIFICATION (1):

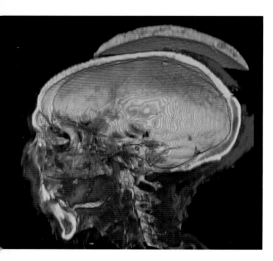

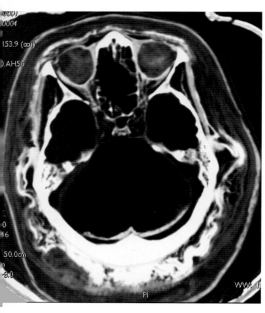

RIGHT Dummy canopic jars such as these were placed in tombs during the Third Intermediate Period, when the internal organs of the body were usually put back inside the chest. 25th Dynasty, about 700 BC. British Museum EA 9562, 9564–5.

The first task which the embalmer performed was the extraction of the brain. The Greek historian Herodotus recorded that, in his day (c.450 BC), this was done via the nose, and examination of many mummies has confirmed this. A small chisel was used to perforate the small bones at the top of the nose, and a metal rod was inserted into the skull cavity. Using this, the brain, which would have partly liquefied already in the hot climate, was drawn in pieces down the nostril and disposed of. The scans of Nesperennub confirm that this method was followed during his mummification. Damage to the ethmoid bone at the top of the nose is visible, and all trace of the brain is gone. However, the 3D images show traces of a thin, papery substance clinging to the inside of the skull at the back of the head – these are almost certainly the remains of the meninges (or membranes that surround the brain), left behind after the process of removal.

Next, the embalmer made an incision on the left side of the abdomen. Through this almost all of the internal organs were removed. The corpse was then covered with natron, a natural compound of salts, which – over a period of about forty days – absorbed all the bodily fluids. Some of the internal organs (usually the liver, lungs, stomach and intestines) were also preserved and wrapped in resin-soaked bandages. For many centuries these bundles were placed in four vessels now called canopic jars, and stored in the tomb in a special niche or close to the coffin. From c.1100 BC to c.700 BC (and often in later centuries) they were simply replaced in the body cavity, each package accompanied by a wax figurine representing one of four protective deities, the sons of Horus.

Other organs were discarded, but the heart was always given special treatment. It was regarded as the centre of the individual's being, both physically and spiritually – hence it was seen as the location of the mind and memory. It was left in its place when all the other contents of the chest were removed.

REMOVING THE
INTERNAL ORGANS

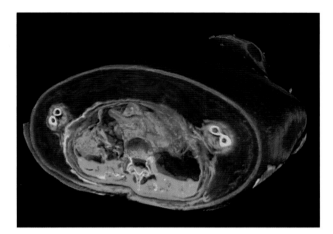

LEFT A clipping plane through the torso, showing the arm bones and the interior of the chest. Solidified resin lies at each side of the spine, and the spaces above are filled with packing and bundles probably containing the internal organs.

CENTRE LEFT Front view of the lower abdomen showing bones and other dense material. The rectangular object lying over the left flank is a metal plate covering the incision made to extract the internal organs.

BELOW Four figurines of resin representing the Sons of Horus. Such images were placed inside the chest of the mummy to give magical protection to the internal organs. Third Intermediate Period, about 1069–664 BC. British Museum EA 15562, 15571, 15579, 15580.

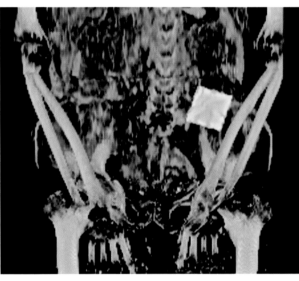

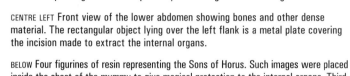

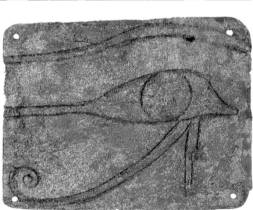

ABOVE Metal incision plate from a mummy. It bears the *wedjat*, or Eye of Horus, a common protective device which symbolically 'healed' the embalming incision. Third Intermediate Period, about 1069–664 BC. British Museum EA 8409.

RIGHT A clipping plane through the front of Nesperennub's mummy revealing the packages containing the internal organs on the right of the chest cavity.

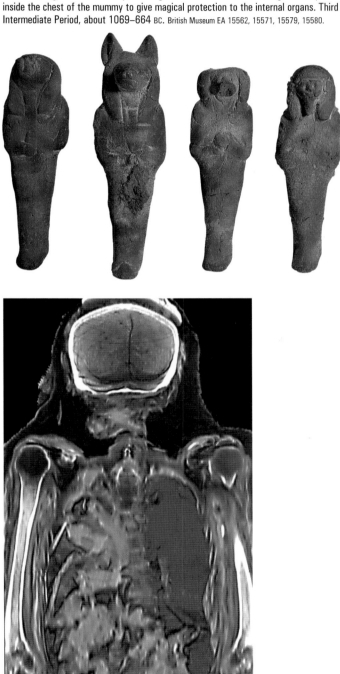

31

MUMMIFICATION (2):

After the preservation of the corpse came the lengthy process of adorning and wrapping it. This often involved placing items of jewellery, amulets and other trappings on the body and between the layers of bandages.

Just beneath Nesperennub's outer wrappings, narrow bands of a relatively low density material can be seen passing over the shoulders and crossing on the chest. At the lower ends are tabs. These objects, known to Egyptologists as stolae or 'mummy-braces', are usually made of leather, dyed red, with terminals of undyed leather with red edging. Gods such as Osiris are often depicted wearing them, and from about 1100 BC they began to be included among the trappings of mummies, perhaps to promote the idea that through the rituals of mummification the dead were elevated to a status similar to that of gods. The braces are common on mummies of the Twenty-first and Twenty-second Dynasties, and are often painted on the coffins and cartonnage cases of this period;

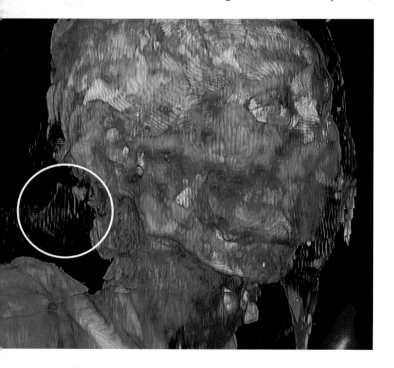

they are shown, for example, on the coffin of Ankhefenkhons (p. 9).

A second pair of tabs is visible at the sides of Nesperennub's neck, and these may be the counterparts of those on the breast. He was also equipped with two other leather pendants of different forms. These can be seen clearly lying on the chest close to the braces. Similar examples found on mummies unwrapped in the nineteenth century had been threaded onto narrow leather thongs. Stola-tabs and pendants are of value to historians. They often bear embossed inscriptions that name

PENDANTS AND RINGS

the king who reigned at the time of the mummy's burial. The 3D images do not tell us whether the tabs on Nesperennub's mummy are inscribed. If they are, and with the development of more sensitive scanning technology, it may be possible one day to read the inscriptions and fix the date of his death precisely.

The CT scans show that Nesperennub wears rings on the fingers of each hand. They are made from a relatively dense material, most probably a metal (perhaps even gold). Rings are among the commonest trappings of mummies. Many were found on the body of Tutankhamun, both on his fingers and in groups within the wrappings. Nesperennub probably wore his rings in life, but their bezels may well carry inscriptions or devices which would help to promote the well-being of the wearer after death.

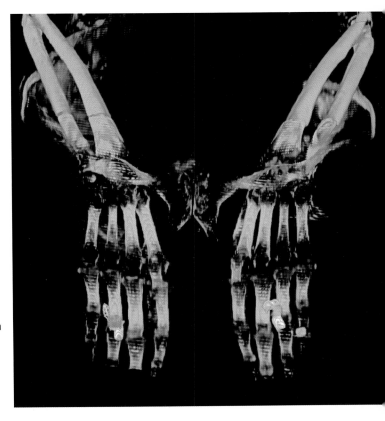

ABOVE Terminal tab of a leather stole from a mummy. It is embossed with an image of King Osorkon I before the goddess Amunet. 22nd Dynasty, about 924–889 BC. British Museum EA 66642.

OPPOSITE TOP The upper layer of wrappings clipped away to expose the leather straps and amulets which lie on the chest.

OPPOSITE BOTTOM Right side of the head. Below the ear is the faint shape (circled) of the terminal tab of a leather stole.

ABOVE Drawing of a pair of leather stoles with amulets threaded on thongs, from a Theban mummy of the 22nd Dynasty.

RIGHT The bones of Nesperennub's hands, showing rings on the fingers.

MUMMIFICATION (3):

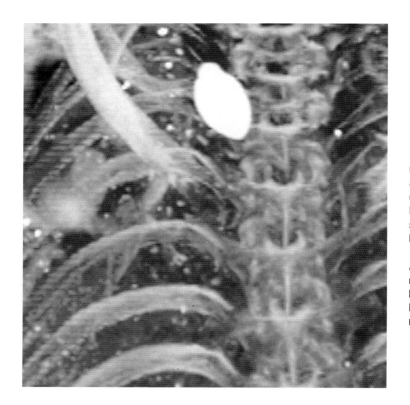

LEFT **A dense object lying above the spine on the chest of Nesperennub. Its shape and position suggest that it is a heart-scarab.**

ABOVE AND RIGHT **Front and rear of a green porphyry heart scarab inscribed for Neskhons. About 1000 BC.** British Museum EA 25584

An important way of giving a person special powers or protection was through the use of amulets. These small images or figurines were usually made of stone, metal or glazed ceramic, and their power was supposed to reside in their shape, their colour, the material they were made from, and any magical texts inscribed on them or spoken over them. Amulets were worn by the living and were often placed on the bodies of the dead, within the wrappings. The mummy of Tutankhamun had a profusion of amulets, and several are visible within the bandages of Nesperennub. The position of the amulets was also important; many were placed on the neck and upper body, regarded by the Egyptians as the most vulnerable areas.

Close to Nesperennub's right collar bone is a roughly oval object made of a dense substance. Shape, size and location suggest that it is a 'heart scarab'. These amulets, usually carved from dark green or black stone, represent the scarab beetle –

a manifestation of the sun god and a symbol of the renewal of life. A magical spell, inscribed on the base in hieroglyphs, commanded the dead man's heart not to reveal any potentially damning information about him when he came into the presence of the gods. It was feared that this might happen during the judgement, which every mortal had to undergo, when the heart was weighed in a balance against an image of right and justice. This weighing would determine whether or not the dead man had lived a good and virtuous life on earth. Only if he had was he judged worthy to enter the afterlife.

On the breast lies a pectoral, probably of sheet metal, in the form of outspread wings. Winged figures were commonly painted on coffins at this period (pp. 8, 9, 15) and pectoral ornaments in similar forms are often seen in the wrappings of mummies. The outline of this example suggests that it represents a winged solar disc, rather than a falcon, vulture or scarab beetle (the most plausible alternatives).

AMULETS ON THE BODY

A group of small amulets is seen clustered at Nesperennub's throat. None of these were visible on the X-rays of the 1960s, and have been revealed for the first time by the new images. Some of them can be recognized instantly by their shape. One is the *djed* pillar, a symbol of the god Osiris, ruler of the realm of the dead. Its function was to magically provide stability and the power to stand up, resurrected. Another is the *wedjat*, or eye of the god Horus. This conferred protection on the wearer, safeguarding him from harm or injury.

Lower down on the breast, just below the winged pectoral, is an object whose shape resembles that of the 'papyrus sceptre' amulet. This represents a sheaf of the papyrus plant bound together in the form of a tall column or staff. It is usually made of greenish glazed faience and its colour as well as its botanical origin symbolize new life by association with the growth of plants.

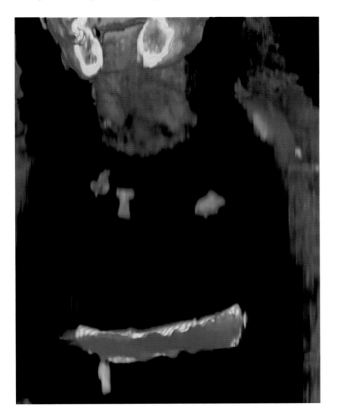

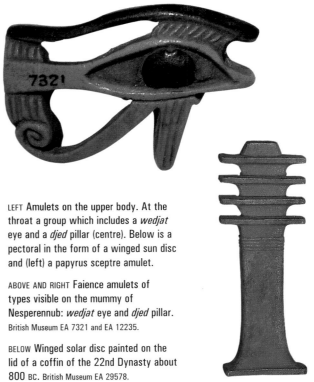

LEFT Amulets on the upper body. At the throat a group which includes a *wedjat* eye and a *djed* pillar (centre). Below is a pectoral in the form of a winged sun disc and (left) a papyrus sceptre amulet.

ABOVE AND RIGHT Faience amulets of types visible on the mummy of Nesperennub: *wedjat* eye and *djed* pillar. British Museum EA 7321 and EA 12235.

BELOW Winged solar disc painted on the lid of a coffin of the 22nd Dynasty about 800 BC. British Museum EA 29578.

MUMMIFICATION (4):

One of the most intriguing features revealed by the 3D images of Nesperennub is a small object in the shape of a snake, which lies just above his right eye. It takes the form of the cobra, the hieroglyphic sign for the sound *dj*. The snake is not simply a flat silhouette, but when viewed from an angle is seen to be a three-dimensional object. However, it does not show up on conventional X-rays and seems to be made of a substance of relatively low density; wax is a possibility, since this was believed by the Egyptians to have magical properties and was used to fashion objects and figurines that were placed on mummies. The object is in very close proximity to the face of Nesperennub, and if not actually in contact with his skin it must be attached to the inner-most layer of wrappings.

An amulet in the form of a snake's head was a fairly common element of the trappings of mummies after the New Kingdom. They are associated with the protection of the throat and their main purpose was probably to ward off snake bites. However, these examples are usually made of a red-coloured material such as jasper. Snake

BELOW CT image of the skull of Nesperennub, showing snake-shaped amulet above the right eye socket.

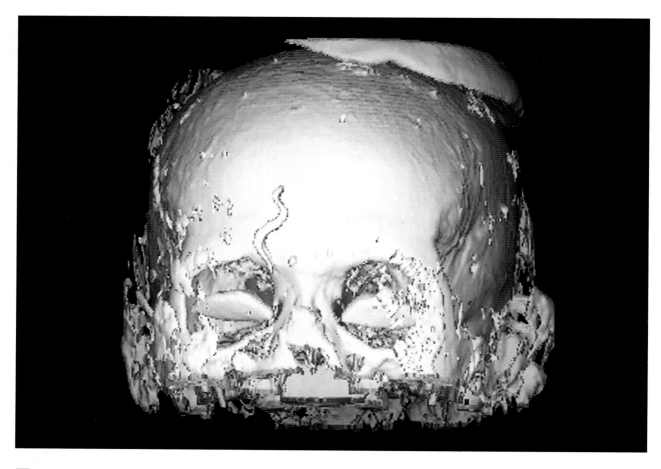

THE SNAKE AMULET

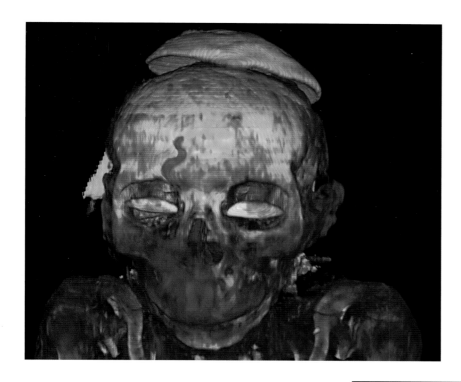

LEFT 3D image of the head, showing skull with remains of soft tissue. The snake amulet appears to be made of a substance which has a relative density between that of flesh and bone; it may be made of wax.

amulets which represent the complete animal are unusual. One made of thin gold was found on the head of the mummy of a priest from Thebes who died about 935 BC, and another has been detected by X-rays over the right eye of a Late Period mummy in the Leiden Museum. Because these snake-amulets are so rare, their precise significance is unknown. The positioning of them on the forehead might possibly suggest some connection with the uraeus serpent. This protective cobra goddess regularly adorned the headdress of the pharaoh, but occasionally appeared on mummies and masks of private individuals. Nesperennub's snake, then, may have had two magical functions – to guard him against evil forces in the afterlife and to suggest that he had gained a higher status in the world of the gods – more akin to that of a king.

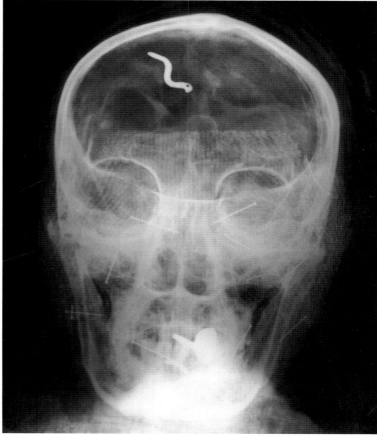

RIGHT X-ray of the skull of a Late Period mummy showing a snake amulet of thin metal, apparently attached to the inner wrappings above the right eye.
Rijksmuseum van Oudheden, Leiden.

THE MYSTERIOUS BOWL:

The cloudy X-ray images obtained in the 1960s had shown that an opaque object lay on the top of Nesperennub's head, underneath the linen wrappings. Gray and Dawson, who drew up the report on the X-rays, thought that this might be a human placenta or afterbirth, which the Egyptians revered as though it were a twin or double of the individual; they claimed to have found a dried placenta on the heads of two other mummies dating to around 1000 BC. However, the new 3D images of Nesperennub immediately revealed that the object on the head was not a placenta, but a shallow bowl of coarse, unfired clay.

The shape of the bowl and the nature of its fabric have been revealed with astonishing clarity. Its irregular form indicates that it was shaped by hand, not on a potter's wheel. There are even impressions in the surface which correspond to the marks of fingers and a thumb.

A clay bowl is a most unusual object to find within the wrappings of a mummy. It does not belong to any known ritual aspect of embalming. The bone of the skull underneath it is not damaged

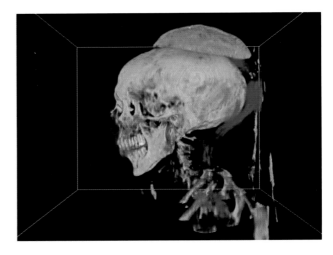

in any way, nor does it seem to be fulfilling any practical purpose. Its crude make points instead to it having been part of the embalmers' working equipment – but why should it have been placed within the wrappings?

When the mummy's head is viewed in 3D from different angles, and under a variety of visualisation settings, an important clue to the bowl's function becomes apparent. Adhering to the top and back of Nesperennub's head, and also to the bowl itself, is what appears to be a thick deposit of some

TOP RIGHT Skull of Nesperennub, showing the clay bowl in contact with the head.

RIGHT A clipping plane through the top of the cartonnage case, showing the position of the bowl on the back of the skull. The coarse fabric of the bowl is clearly visible.

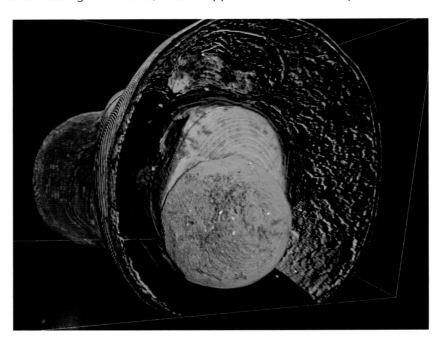

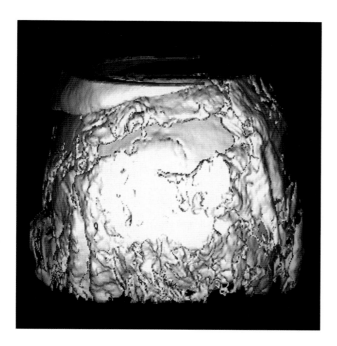 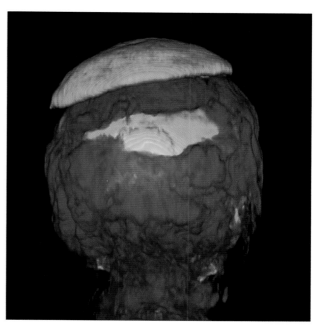

ABOVE LEFT CT image showing large quantities of solidified liquid, probably resin, which collected at the back of the head, partially covering the clay bowl and cementing it to the skull.

ABOVE Deposits of resinous material on the back of the head of Nesperennub. The area of exposed skull may have resulted from an attempt to prise away the solidified mass.

glutinous matter. Its density and its appearance suggest that it is a thick, semi-liquid substance which has solidified. It is probably resin, which was used extensively in mummification. The resin, collected from trees or plants, would be heated until molten and then smeared or brushed over the skin. The clay bowl may have been used by the embalmers to hold some of this resin. Large quantities seem to have been poured over Nesperennub while he lay on the embalming bed, and much of it ran down and began to solidify at the back of his head. Perhaps the embalmers placed the bowl on the head to collect some of this surplus liquid. An experiment using a facsimile of the bowl has shown that it could easily have rested at the back of the head while the body lay supine.

What happened then we do not know. Perhaps the resin hardened unexpectedly quickly, cementing the bowl firmly to the skull. Discovering their mistake, the embalmers would surely have tried to remove the bowl. An area on the back of the head from which the skin appears to have been torn away may represent an unsuccessful attempt to prise off the lumps of resin that anchored the bowl in place. Realising that the bowl could not be removed without causing further damage, the embalmers may have decided to proceed with the wrapping of the body, hoping that their mistake would pass unnoticed. It would not be the first or the last time that Egyptian embalmers made errors. Investigations of other mummies have revealed that parts of the body were sometimes lost or displaced, that small tools and probes were left behind inside the corpse (the nightmare of the modern surgeon), and that insects and even small rodents obtained free access to the dead. Since Nesperennub's relatives would not have been present during his mummification, this particular piece of professional negligence would remain a secret for 2,800 years.

WRAPPING THE BODY

Wrapping the body was a very important part of the mummification process. Not only did it ensure that all the essential parts of the corpse remained together, it also helped to create the correct appearance for the dead person. The distinctive mummy shape and the outer trappings emphasized the idea that the deceased had been transformed into an eternal being, one who possessed the attributes of powerful gods. The wrappings of the mummy were even supposed to be made by the gods themselves. Inscriptions refer to the dead person receiving wrappings from Tayet, goddess of weaving, or from the weavers of the goddess Neith.

Linen, made from the flax plant, was the commonest textile used by the ancient Egyptians. Clothes and bedcovers were usually woven from linen, and these items were often recycled as mummy wrappings. Both complete sheets and long strips like bandages were used for wrapping the dead. The amount of linen used varied; one mummy was wrapped in over 375 square metres of cloth.

CT scans of Nesperennub clearly show the many layers of wrappings put on by the embalmers.

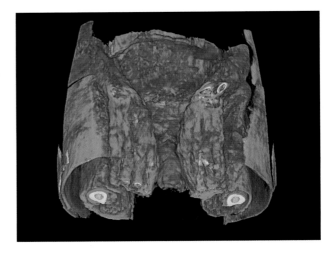

Those closest to the body would be soaked in molten resin to help them to stick to the skin. The usual procedure was for the head, arms and legs to be individually wrapped first. After this, large sheets would alternate with more layers of bandages. The final layer was a single sheet or shroud, covering the whole body. This would often be dyed a reddish pink colour – perhaps to suggest that the dead person was reborn through the life-giving power of the sun god.

In the most elaborate embalming, putting on the wrappings was done with great ceremony. An Egyptian text known as the 'Ritual of Embalming' records the key steps and explains that each piece of cloth had special religious significance. Besides the bandages, amulets were placed between the layers of cloth, and at some periods a papyrus scroll containing religious texts was inserted among the wrappings.

ABOVE RIGHT View of the lower torso, showing the outer layer of wrappings and the surface of the body. The hands of Nesperennub lie on his thighs, and the section through the legs shows the skin, bones and subcutaneous tissue.

BELOW In this view, the cartonnage case has been removed to reveal the outer linen wrappings of the mummy.

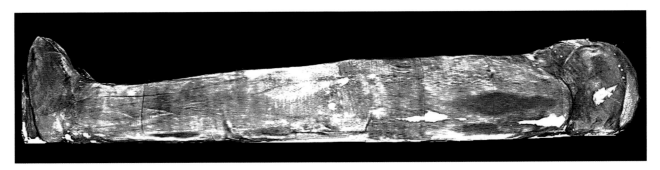

ABOVE Examples of linen
mummy wrappings.
British Museum EA 6516, 6518, 6542.

BELOW Stages in the wrapping of a mummy of the Third Intermediate Period.
Left to right: the first wrappings are placed under the mummy and the head
is covered (note incision plate on left flank); the torso and limbs are
individually wrapped, and amulets put in place; the limbs are confined within
broad strips of linen; the outermost shroud is held in place by retaining bands.

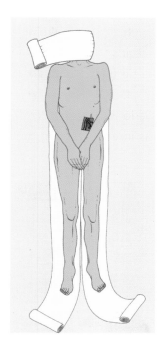
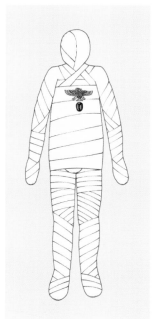
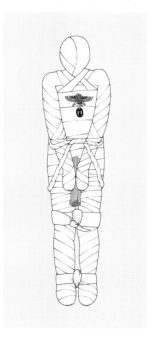
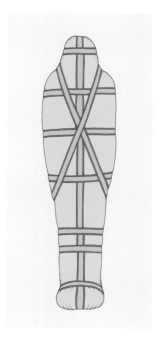

CONSTRUCTING THE CARTONNAGE CASE

Once wrapping had been completed, the mummy was put into a coffin – often, indeed, into two, three or even four coffins – one inside the other. Egyptian coffins were usually made of wood or stone, and were either rectangular or carved to imitate the shape of the mummy. The majority consisted of two parts – a lid and a case to hold the body. But in the ninth and eighth centuries BC, when Nesperennub lived, inner coffins were often made of *cartonnage*, a laminate of linen and plaster. Layers of cloth were carefully built up around a disposable core, probably of mud and straw, which reproduced the shape of the mummy. When complete, the core was removed, leaving a tough shell of linen. The mummy was put inside this through an opening at the back, and the two flaps were drawn together and tightly laced with string, like a shoe. A coating of fine white plaster was applied to the outer surface, and inscriptions and religious images painted

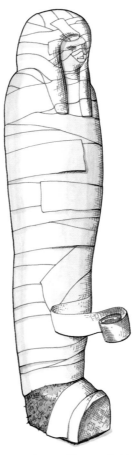
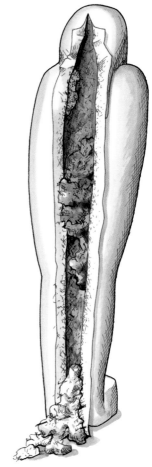

Construction of a cartonnage mummy case:
1. A mummy-shaped core is constructed from mud mixed with straw, perhaps built around a lightweight frame of reeds.

2. Up to twenty layers of linen soaked in glue or plaster are applied to the core, closely following its shape.

3. While the linen layers are still pliable, the core material is extracted in pieces through an opening in the back.

on. The advantages of this type of coffin were that it was cheaper and easier to make than one of stone or wood, and that once the mummy was sealed inside, it could not be removed again without damaging the painted case. This was a precaution against thieves, who sometimes stole coffins and sold them to new purchasers after erasing the name of the original owner. This unscrupulous practice was widespread among cemetery employees at Thebes about 1000–900 BC, and might have contributed to the growing popularity of cartonnage cases. They ensured that the dead person inside the case would not be deprived of the all-important religious imagery painted on the surface, and they also preserved the name – regarded by the Egyptians as a key element of the human being, which must survive if he/she was to enter the afterlife.

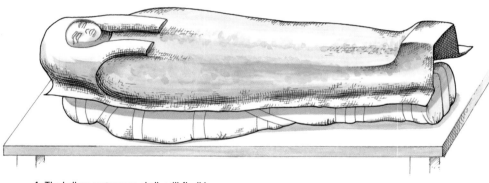

4. The hollow cartonnage shell, still flexible, is fitted around the wrapped mummy, and the rear flaps drawn together.

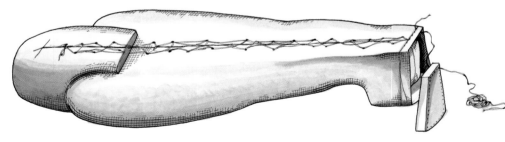

5. Cord is threaded through holes punched along the rear edges, and the mummy is secured inside. The open foot-end of the case is sealed with a wooden board, attached with pegs or cord.

6. When the cartonnage has dried and hardened, painted decoration is applied to the exterior over a ground of fine white plaster.

COFFINS: DECORATION

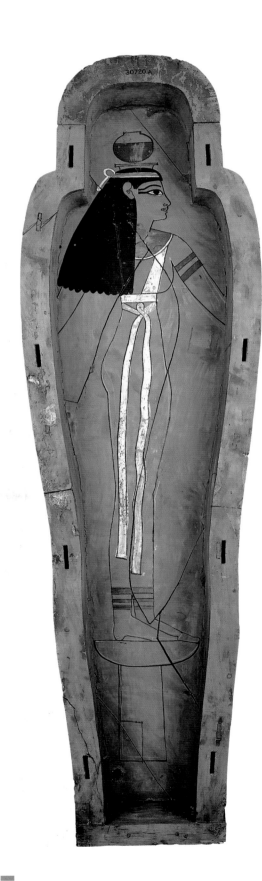

Besides providing physical protection for the corpse, Egyptian coffins were supposed to equip the occupant with magical attributes and ritual knowledge to assist him/her on the passage into the afterlife. This role was expressed through the shape and colouring of the coffins, and through the texts and images on their surfaces. At some periods of Egyptian history the most important of these details were put on the walls of the tomb chapel or on papyrus rolls buried with the mummy. But at the time in which Nesperennub lived very few decorated tombs were being made for private individuals, and funerary papyri were no longer in use, so the surfaces of the coffins became the main vehicle for displaying religious images and writings. Because of the limited space available, images were carefully designed to convey different levels of meaning simultaneously.

The 'anthropoid', or mummiform, shape of the coffin reflected the divine status which the dead attained. Nesperennub's outer wooden coffin is simple in design, with a painted face, wig and collar and a line of inscription identifying the occupant. The reddish colouring of the background associates the deceased with the sun god.

The coffin was also regarded symbolically as a kind of cocoon. Inside, the dead person lay like a child in its mother's womb, ready to be reborn into the afterlife. Figures of important goddesses, such as Nut or Hathor, were often painted on the inside of the coffin. These images often have their arms outstretched to enfold the mummy in a protective embrace, emphasising the maternal aspect.

The main concentration of religious images was usually put on to the inner coffin, in close proximity to the mummy, and this applies to the cartonnage case of Nesperennub. He is surrounded by figures of gods and religious symbols, carefully arranged according to an underlying plan which would help to bring about Nesperennub's rebirth and eternal life.

On the breast is a scarab with the head and wings of a

LEFT Interior of Nesperennub's wooden coffin. On the floor is painted the figure of a goddess, whose arms extend on to the side walls in a symbolic gesture of protection. The jar-hieroglyph above her head indicates that she is Nut, the sky goddess and mother of Osiris, although her feet rest on a hieroglyphic group signifying the name of the goddess Nephthys. British Museum EA 30720.

LEFT The upper section of the cartonnage case, on which is depicted the sun god as a scarab beetle with a falcon's head and wings. Below, two serpent goddesses and the four Sons of Horus flank a mummified falcon representing the funerary god Sokar-Osiris. British Museum EA 30720.

falcon. The scarab beetle, Khepri represented the sun at dawn, while the falcon was more closely associated with the daytime sun. Beneath are two pairs of gods in mummy-shape representing the Sons of Horus, whose names were Imsety, Hapy, Duamutef and Qebhsennuef. They protected the internal organs of the mummy, but they were also believed to help raise the sun god into the sky each morning. For this reason they are positioned here below his wings. Two snakes, facing the Sons of Horus, represent goddesses who protected the sun god. In the centre of this band is a mummified falcon representing Sokar, a very ancient god associated with the city of Memphis. He was often linked with Ptah and Osiris, to form a composite deity who promoted the resurrection of the dead.

The central image of the lower zone is a fetish, or emblem, which stands for Osiris, the chief god of the netherworld. It is mounted on a pole and is topped by ostrich feathers. The original fetish was kept in the temple of Osiris at Abydos, where it was

RIGHT The lower section is dominated by the domed and feathered fetish of Abydos, emblem of the god Osiris, which is flanked by ram-standards, winged goddesses and falcons. British Museum EA 30720.

surrounded by standards and images of deities. Two of these, bearing ram-figures, are shown on the mummy-case of Nesperennub. Each standard is supported by an *ankh*, the sign of life, which is provided with human arms. Through the painting of the fetish on the mummy-case, the dead person was closely identified with Osiris. Just as the god was believed to have risen from the dead, so Nesperennub would be restored to life for eternity.

At each side of the Osiris emblem stand the goddesses Isis and Nephthys. They were the sisters of the murdered Osiris who, according to mythology, restored him to life by beating the air with their wings. Here their winged arms convey life and at the same time shield the god's emblem from harm. Below, further protection is provided by two falcons. Although not named here, they are identified on similar mummy-cases as the goddesses Neith and Selkis. At the lower extremity of the case are two jackals representing the god Wepwawet, whose name means the 'Opener of the Ways.' His role was to protect the dead and to guide their footsteps on their passage to the next world – a duty which is reflected in the positioning of these figures at the feet.

The two most important elements of this design are the winged sun god and the emblem of Osiris. Each of these deities was believed to have the power to renew life, and each ruled over a different part of the universe: the sun god's realm was in the sky, and that of Osiris beneath the earth. Every night the two were momentarily joined and rejuvenated, and at dawn the sun god rose reborn into the sky, symbolising new life for all. The positioning of the winged sun god above the Osiris emblem was meant to symbolize the rising of the sun out of the netherworld. This pairing of images therefore suggests the dawning of a new day, a metaphor for renewed life.

Lastly, on the wooden board beneath the mummy's feet is painted the galloping pied bull Apis. This was the sacred animal of the creator god Ptah of Memphis. One of its roles was to carry the dead on his back to their tombs, and this explains why it is shown here.

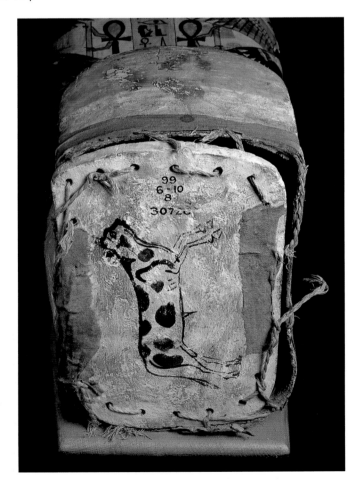

BELOW On the footboard of the cartonnage case is an image of the Apis bull, a manifestation of the god Ptah of Memphis. One of his functions was to carry the dead to their tombs, and on later coffins this motif includes an image of the mummy borne on the bull's back. British Museum EA 30720.

THE FUTURE:
THE MUMMY IN CYBERSPACE

Through the meeting of the museum world with that of leading-edge computer technology, the secrets of life, death and mummification in ancient Egypt can now be presented to the public in an exciting new way, revealing more than could ever be discovered through unwrapping, while preserving a priceless historical resource intact. And investigators need not be restricted to working in an immersive theatre to find out more. Using an SGI developed technique called 'Visual Serving', a standard desktop client such as a conventional PC can also be connected remotely to the SGI visualisation supercomputer, and can view the data interactively across a network.

Nesperennub, the first mummy to be examined in its entirety in this way, is a pioneer, beckoning the investigator to new horizons. With even higher resolution images and refined visualisation tools we will see what lies within with even greater clarity. By applying this technology to other ancient bodies, scientists will vastly increase the potential yield of data about past populations. Treated non-invasively and with respect, ancient human remains will lead us on to new levels of understanding.

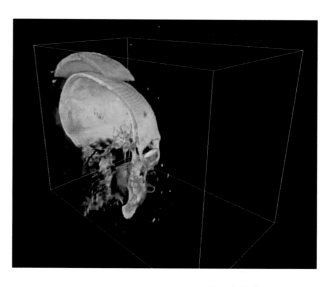

ABOVE AND BELOW LEFT The skull of Nesperennub, isolated within a 'virtual cell' and sectioned using clipping planes.

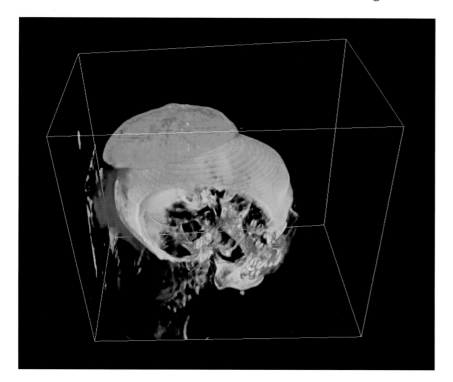

Further reading

Taylor, J. H., *Death and the Afterlife in Ancient Egypt* (London, 2001).

Dodson, A. and Ikram, S., *The Mummy in Ancient Egypt* (London, 1998).

David, R., and Archbold, R., *Conversations with Mummies* (London, 2000).

Aufderheide, A., *The Scientific Study of Mummies* (Cambridge, 2003).

Gray, P. H. K., and Dawson, W. R., *Catalogue of Egyptian Antiquities in the British Museum*, I. *Mummies and Human Remains* (London, 1968).

Acknowledgements

This project is the result of a long-term collaboration between the British Museum and SGI, and thanks are due to Mark Westaby and the staff at Portfolio Communications for bringing this about. The concept and its development owe an immense amount to the commitment and enthusiasm of David Hughes and to the technical expertise and problem-solving acumen of Tom Fuke of SGI. Thanks are also due to Sam Hughes, whose idea of presenting the project to his school class was crucial in revealing its huge potential as an educational experience.

The National Hospital for Neurology and Neurosurgery, London, generously provided CT scanning facilities. The development of the 3D dataset was the work of Tom Fuke, Andrew Preece, Gareth Morgan and Colin Middleton, all of SGI. Richard Bibb and Dominic Eggbeer of The National Centre for Product Design and Development Research, Cardiff, created stereolithographic replicas of the skull of Nesperennub, and Dr Caroline Wilkinson of the University of Manchester made the facial reconstruction. Margaret Judd, Simon Hillson and Nigel Strudwick provided invaluable advice and assistance. Thanks are also due to Charlotte Mounter of British Museum Press for editing the text and seeing the book through the press.

Picture credits

All illustrations are © The British Museum, except where stated otherwise.

Claire Thorne: drawings pp.14, 33, 41, 42-3.

John H. Taylor: pp.8 (bottom), 11 (top), 12 (bottom), 18 (middle).

Map of Thebes p.9 and Plan of the temples of Karnak p.11: based on I. Shaw and P. Nicholson, *British Museum Dictionary of Ancient Egypt* (London, 1995).

Manchester Museum: p.16 (bottom).

National Hospital for Neurology and Neurosurgery: pp.18 (bottom), 19 (top left), 29 (bottom), 30 (middle), 34 (top left), 36, 39 (left).

Phoebe Apperson Hearst Museum of Anthropology and the Regents of the University of California: p15.

Photographic imagery courtesy of SGI: front (skeleton) and back cover images, p.6, p.19 (top right and bottom right), pp.20-21), p.22 (top and bottom left), p.23, p.26 (left), p.27, p.28, p.29 (top), p.30 (top), p.31 (top, middle left and bottom right), p.32, p.33 (bottom right), p.35 (left), p.37 (top), p.38, p.39 (right), p.40 (top).

St Thomas' Hospital: p.17 (top right).

University of Manchester: pp.24-5.

View of Thebes p.10 (bottom): from S. Aufrere, J.-Cl. Golvin and J.-C. Goyon, *Egypte restituée* (Paris, 1994-7).

JUN · 2005